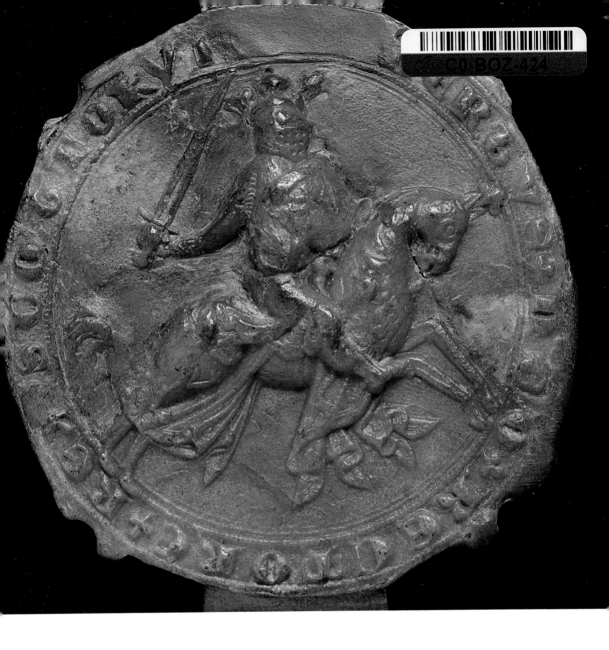

ROBERT the BRUCE

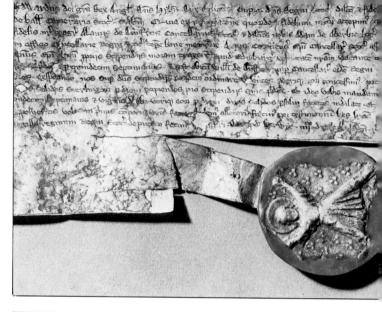

TOP RIGHT: *Warrant of Edward I as overlord of Scotland, 4 July 1292. In return for agreeing to decide on the successor to Margaret of Norway, the English king demanded recognition as overlord and the Guardians acknowledged him as such on 13 June 1291. In this warrant Edward I authorises payment of expenses to Alan of Dumfries, Chancellor of Scotland, and uses the Guardians' seal: St Andrew extended on his cross with the legend "Andrea Scotis dux esto compatriotis" ("Andrew, be a guide to the Scots, your fellow-countrymen").*
LEFT: *Seal of John Balliol, showing him seated on the throne (above) and as mounted warrior (below). Edward chose the compliant Balliol as king and then treated him as his vassal. Eventually*

Balliol turned to France for support. A furious Edward entered Scotland in 1296, asserted his military presence at the main castles, and at the battle of Dunbar defeated Balliol, who was deprived of his kingdom and even the royal arms on his coat—hence the name "Toom Tabard" ("Empty Coat").
ABOVE: *The Ragman Rolls. Edward I, "Hammer of the Scots", obliged 2,000 Scottish nobles to formally recognise him as their king by putting their seals on this document in October 1296.*
FACING PAGE: *William Wallace, as seen through Victorian eyes. While the deposed Balliol enjoyed the relative safety of the Tower of London a Scottish revolt was organised in 1297 by Wallace. This statue was erected in Aberdeen in 1888.*

ROBERT the BRUCE

Alan Bold

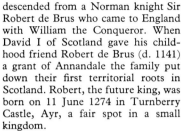

THE life of Robert the Bruce contains many of those rare moments in history when personal ambition coincides completely with national aspiration. Because of Edward I's reduction of Scotland to a vassal kingdom Bruce's pursuit of a crown made him also the heroic leader of a national war of liberation. The culmination of his struggle, the great victory at Bannockburn, achieved so much and in such a manner that it inspired the three most eloquently patriotic passages in Scottish literature: The Declaration of Arbroath; John Barbour's assertion that "fredome is a noble thing!" in *The Bruce*; and Burns's poetic version of Bruce's pre-battle speech to his troops at Bannockburn, "Scots, Wha Hae". Bannockburn was not merely an isolated victory: it was a national triumph.

Scotland's greatest patriot king was

descended from a Norman knight Sir Robert de Brus who came to England with William the Conqueror. When David I of Scotland gave his childhood friend Robert de Brus (d. 1141) a grant of Annandale the family put down their first territorial roots in Scotland. Robert, the future king, was born on 11 June 1274 in Turnberry Castle, Ayr, a fair spot in a small kingdom.

In the 13th century the population of Scotland was around half a million, which is the present population of Edinburgh. The nobility, from the earls downward (and Robert's father, 6th lord of Annandale, became 1st earl of Carrick by marriage), formed the *communitas regni Scotie*—"community of the realm of Scotland"—and were feudally obliged to perform military service for their king. That is, when they had one.

In 1286 King Alexander III, night-riding from Edinburgh to join his newly-acquired second wife, toppled to his death over the Kinghorn cliffs. His abrupt death left, as successor to the throne, his 3-year-old granddaughter Margaret of Norway in whose absence six Guardians were appointed as collective caretakers of the Scottish kingdom. As the elegiac author of the earliest recorded piece of Scottish poetry recognised, Scotland's golden age came to a dead end when Alexander III took his fatal tumble:

> Sen Alexander our king wes deid
> That Scotland left in luve and lee,
> Away wes sonse of aill and breid,
> Of wine and wax, of gamin and glee.
> The gold wes changit all in leid,
> The frute failyeit on everilk tree.
> Christ succour Scotland and remeid
> That stad is in perplexitie.

England's Edward I, a mature statesman of 47, took advantage of the Scottish political crisis to arrange, by the 1290 Treaty of Birgham, a marriage between the Maid of Norway (then 7) and his 6-year-old son Edward. Though the treaty accepted that Scotland was to remain "separate and divided from the kingdom of England" Edward I had other ideas in mind. In October came news of another royal death: the Maid of Norway had perished in

Orkney on her voyage over. Thirteen competitors laid claim to her vacant throne. Of these there were two clear frontrunners, both descended from David I's son Henry of Northumberland: the future King Robert's grandfather Robert Bruce, 5th lord of Annandale; and John Balliol, lord of Galloway.

To make their minds up for them the Guardians of Scotland invited none other than the subduer of Wales, Edward I, who now made his intentions absolutely clear by announcing at the Anglo-Scottish parliament of Norham in May 1291 that he had come in his capacity as "the superior and lord paramount of the kingdom of Scotland" and must be formally acknowledged as such. This the *communitas* could not accept so Edward I instead persuaded seven of the competitors to acknowledge him as their feudal superior and overlord of Scotland. Competitors Bruce and John Balliol both accepted Edward I's terms.

Competitor Bruce, now an old man, decided on 7 November 1292 to transfer his royal claim to his son Robert who in turn passed the earldom of Carrick to his 18-year-old son Robert, the future king. It made little difference. A decision was given in favour of John Balliol who duly acknowledged Edward I as his overlord and then, after a traditional coronation at Scone, went to Newcastle to do homage to his English lord and master. As he began so he continued. Balliol's three-year reign is a tale of appeasement. Edward I insisted on his right to hear legal appeals from Scotland and when Balliol protested he was imperiously summoned to London where he had to reaffirm that he was indeed vassal of the English king.

Things changed, however, when Edward I declared war against Philip IV of France on 24 June 1294 and demanded military service from his vassals in Wales and Scotland. Under Madog ap Llywelyn the Welsh formed a resistance movement while the Scots, lacking a patriotic hero, evolved a council of twelve nobles to motivate Balliol into defiance of the English king. The Bruce family had little inclination to serve Balliol's interests

L Robert Bruce began his Raigne(?) 1306

Isabel rychts oye [Earl of] Marr

his control of their kingdom. Yet this moment of national humiliation a champion emerged.

William Wallace of Elderslie, Renfrewshire, seemed to appear from nowhere in 1297 to galvanise anti English feeling and turn it into an organised revolt. He murdered the English sheriff of Lanark, then carried out a raid on an English court at Scone. Although it was clearly against his selfish interests to oppose Edward (who had restored the earldom Balliol had confiscated) Robert Bruce, 2nd earl of Carrick, decided to join the Scottish rebels while his father, lord of Annandale, maintained his support of the English. Bruce himself explained his political conversion thus: "I must join my own people and the nation in which I was born."

Using brilliant military tactics Wallace trapped and defeated the English at Stirling Bridge in 1297 and assumed the title Guardian of Scotland. However Edward I did not earn his title "*Malleus Scottorum*" ("Hammer of the Scots") for nothing. At Falkirk on 22 July 1298 he defeated the Scots so badly that Wallace resigned the Guardianship and went underground. His place was taken by two joint Guardians: Robert the Bruce and Toom Tabard's nephew John "Red" Comyn, lord of Badenoch. With such intense family rivalry friction was inevitable and, at a war council at Peebles in August 1299, Comyn was literally at Bruce's throat. It was an insult Bruce would pay back with injury.

Bruce's place as Guardian was taken by Ingram de Umfraville in 1300 so he must have entered the 14th century with some doubts as to where his future lay. Even though Wallace's ostensible aim was the restoration of the exiled Toom Tabard his brief leadership of the Scottish rebels exhilarated young men like Bruce. With Wallace in hiding the fight for an independent Scotland seemed futile to Bruce if the end-product was simply to be the triumph of the Balliol Comyn family interests at the expense of his own. Accordingly in 1302 Bruce formally submitted to the English who, in return for his services, guaranteed "life and limb, lands and tenements" and granted a pardon. As if to cement his new bond with the English, Bruce married Elizabeth de Burgh, daughter of Edward I's follower the earl of Ulster. This was Bruce's second marriage: his first, to

and when competitor Bruce died in 1295 his son and grandson remained loyal to Edward I, on whose side they were ranged as the wars of independence began. For this they were deprived of their lands by the ineffectual Balliol.

*   *   *

However the choice of father and son Bruce was a practical one. In response to Balliol's resistance Edward I invaded Scotland in 1296, taking Berwick, then Dunbar, then Brechin, where Balliol's abject resignation of his kingdom to Edward I earned him the ignominious nickname "Toom Tabard" ("Empty Coat") because the royal arms were stripped from his tunic. Back at Berwick Edward I had 2,000 Scottish nobles put their seals to the Ragman Rolls as recognition of sabella, daughter of Donald, earl f Mar, produced a daughter Marjory, ʾho in turn produced the first Stuart ing.

Meanwhile Edward I was eliminat-ʌg all pockets of resistance and on 24 august 1305 he had William Wallace rutally executed as the grisly culmi-ation of his intense campaign against he Scots. After avoiding capture for even years Wallace had been betrayed ʌear Glasgow. He was taken to Lon-lon, tried at Westminster Hall for reason (though he had never acknow-edged Edward I as his king), dragged ɔ Smithfield where he was hung, lrawn, quartered and beheaded. To liscourage the others Edward I had Vallace's piked head displayed on ∟ondon Bridge while the four bits of ʌis mutilated body were sent to Newcastle, Berwick, Stirling and ʾerth.

Edward I no doubt believed that ʌis Scottish troubles were over with ʾhis violent liquidation of the main ymbol of Scottish resistance. Yet Edward I's judicial murder of Wallace vas soon to be outdone by another act ɔf violence, this time a sacrilegious murder.

Bruce knew that "Red" John Comyn of Badenoch, the exiled Balliol's nephew, was an obstacle that ʌad to be cleared from his path to the Scottish throne (and with the death of ʾhis father in 1304 Bruce had inherited a legitimate claim). If Comyn would not be an ally then he was much too formidable to be tolerated as an enemy. As joint Guardian Comyn had competed with Bruce for power, in-fluence and prestige. His pedigree was impeccable. He had friends, in-cluding English friends, in high places. Still, Comyn himself must have been more than curious about the current position of Robert Bruce, earl of Carrick, who had first been converted to the cause of Scottish independence and then converted back to a pro-English position.

So on 10 February 1306 Comyn agreed to Bruce's request for a meet-ing in the Franciscan church of Greyfriars in Dumfries. Standing in front of the high altar the two men talked politics and rebellion until it became apparent to Comyn that Bruce's fervour was inspired, not by the religious setting, but by ambition. Comyn could have Bruce's lands, it was proposed, in return for helping to restore an independent Scottish monarchy under Bruce. So uncom-

promisingly fierce was Comyn's re-jection of this proposal that Bruce forgot where he was: he drew his dagger and stabbed the lord of Badenoch. Following their leader's example Bruce's followers finished Comyn off and struck down Sir Robert Comyn when he came forward to defend his wounded nephew.

Bruce had not only murdered an important powerfully-connected noble but had done it in a church. In such circumstances his cause seemed utterly hopeless. He had, at the stroke of a dagger, put himself outside the law

ABOVE: *The coronation chair in West-minster Abbey. Enclosed within it is the Stone of Scone, which according to tradition was brought to Scotland by Fergus of Dalriada around 500. Since 843, when Kenneth MacAlpin was crowned king of a united Scotland at the sacred Pictish centre of Scone, the Stone of Destiny had symbolised the continuity of the Scottish monarchy. At Bruce's coronation at Scone on 27 March 1306 the stone was conspicuous by its absence: it had been taken to Westminster Abbey by Edward I, who had captured it during his victorious invasion of Scotland in 1296, and there it was to remain.*

and would have to live as a landless fugitive unless he took the seemingly impossible alternative and claimed the throne of Scotland. Thus he decided that his only chance of survival was to draw his strength, as Wallace had done, from the anti-English elements in the country. Unlike Wallace, though, he would act on his own behalf. His mind was virtually made up for him. Six weeks after the sacrilegious murder of Comyn he was, at least nominally, king of Scotland.

Even Bruce's wife confessed to feeling of hopelessness at his decision to claim a kingdom when she told him "Alas, we are but King and Queen of the May." As for the English, when they were not treating him as a murderous bogeyman they verbally cut him down to size by calling him King "Hob" (a diminutive lacking the dignity of "Robert"). The odds against Bruce keeping a kingdom were absolutely enormous: Edward I's army and hold on Scotland; the virulent hostility of an outraged papacy; the might and seething moral indignation of the murdered Comyn's kinsmen in Lorne and Buchan. Yet Bruce went ahead with his coronation.

This took place at Scone on 25 March 1306 and was symbolic of the battered state of the Scottish nation. The traditional Crowning Stone had been stolen by Edward I and he would sooner have smashed it on Bruce's head than return it. Bishop Robert Wishart of Glasgow Cathedral not only had to see Bruce crowned but had to antagonise his spiritual masters by absolving Bruce from the excommunication imposed by Pope Clement V on the sacrilegious murderer of

*   *   *

ABOVE LEFT: *At Bruce's coronation a gold coronet was placed on his head by Isabella, countess of Buchan. The new Scottish king, almost 32, must have appeared as he does in C. d'O. Pilkington Jackson's sculptured head which was modelled from a cast of Bruce's skull.*

LEFT: *The Brooch of Lorne. The defeat of Bruce on 19 June 1306 at Methven, Perth, by the earl of Pembroke made a hunted outlaw of the recently crowned Scottish king and it took all his courage and cunning to avoid capture. On 11 August 1306 Bruce was almost caught by the MacDougalls of Lorne at Dalry near Tyndrum and, it is said, one MacDougall clansman was killed with the king's brooch in his grasp.*

ohn Comyn. The earl of Fife, hereditary crowner of Scotland's kings, was under Edward I's orders not to attend. So a second coronation had to be held on 27 March at which the earl's sister Countess Isabella of Buchan placed a gold coronet on Bruce's head.

Edward I appointed Aymer de Valence, Comyn's brother-in-law, to deal with Bruce, which he did, effectively, at the pitched battle of Methven on 19 June 1306. With his few remaining followers Bruce headed west where, in August, he was almost captured at Dalry near Tyndrum by the MacDougalls of Lorne who, as Comyn's kinsmen, were doubly dangerous enemies. Bruce was a powerful and formidable fighter, though, and he managed to escape. Not, however, before one clansman got near enough to grasp Bruce's shoulder clasp-brooch. The fugitive king killed his assailant but had to leave his brooch in the dead man's grasp.

Fearing for the safety of his family Bruce sent his womenfolk to Kildrummy Castle in Aberdeenshire while he and some 200 followers took to the Breadalbane hills of Perthshire. He had been outlawed by Edward I, excommunicated by Clement V and now, in September, he was to be deprived of family. Kildrummy Castle had been taken: brother Neil was hung, drawn and beheaded; sister Mary and Countess Isabella of Buchan were stuck in cages; Bruce's wife and daughter were put in separate prisons. Bruce himself was enough of a realist to admit that his present position in Scotland was quite hopeless. Escape became an obsessive necessity. Moving south-westerly he reached Dunaverty Castle in Kintyre and from there sailed 14 miles to the island of Rathlin off the Irish coast. From September 1306 until his return to the Scottish mainland his movements are unknown so that tales of visits as far afield as Norway are, like his legendary contemplation of the persistence of the spider, matters of conjecture.

What is certain is that Bruce returned to his earldom of Carrick in February 1307 to find it confiscated by the enemy. His own tenants were, understandably, afraid to come out

*　　　*　　　*

RIGHT: *Buttress statues of Edward I and his queen, Eleanor of Castile, at Lincoln Cathedral.*

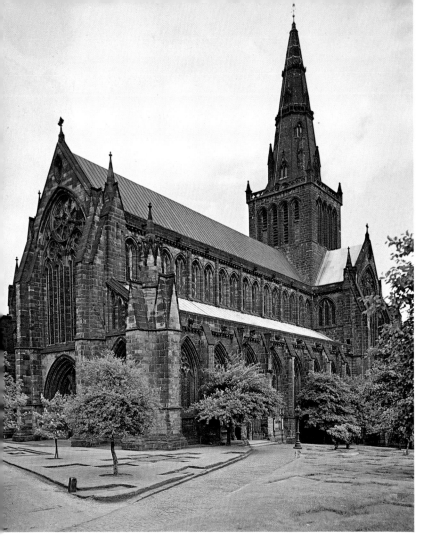

to Ayr. With these victories to encourage him Bruce must have felt he had God himself on his side when he heard a dramatic piece of news from England.

On 7 July 1307 Edward I, aged 68 died at Burgh-on-Sands at the Solway Firth. According to tradition the dying wish of Edward I, belligerent to the last, was that his bones should be carried before his army until Scotland was conquered. Bruce is supposed to have commented that he did indeed fear the bones of Edward I more than the presence of Edward II.

The new English king was 23, an accomplished sportsman and patron of the arts, but not, clearly not, made for war. Edward II did not choose to begin his reign by attempting to emulate his father's hammering of the Scots. So he stayed at home. He further played into Bruce's hand by replacing the formidable de Valence as lieutenant of Scotland by John of Britanny. Bruce was thus left relatively free first to consolidate the ground his victories had gained, then to set about establishing himself in the pro-Balliol territories of Buchan Argyll and Galloway.

Yet when this period of civil war opened he was almost defeated by illness. He had to be carried on a litter to Inverurie. There John Comyn, earl of Buchan, found him apparently at his mercy. What brought the king from his sickbed was the distressing news that some of his men had been slaughtered in a surprise attack. Still in the flush of his astonishing recovery from what seemed a fatal illness Bruce put himself at the head of his 700-strong army and, on 24 December 1307, put Buchan's army to flight at Inverurie. Nor did Bruce forget to exact revenge for the antipathy of the area. The countryside of Buchan was savaged and the people of Buchan were subdued.

Next big target for Bruce was Argyll. And he was expected. John MacDougall of Lorne, lord of Argyll, determined to borrow Bruce's fighting tactics by mounting an ambush in the narrow Pass of Brander. MacDougall's men would be waiting on the slopes of Cruachan to fall on Bruce's army as they arrived at the Pass. Instead MacDougall was caught in his own trap simply because Bruce was always several tactical steps ahead of his adversaries. The Scottish king sent James Douglas and a Highland force further still up the slopes of

openly in his support. It became clear to Bruce that his only chance of success lay in avoiding pitched battles with the English who would always have the advantage in man-power and military equipment. Instead Bruce

*   *   *

ABOVE: *Glasgow Cathedral. The Bishop of Glasgow, Robert Wishart, was one of the most consistently patriotic voices in Scotland: he supported Wallace, absolved Bruce after Pope Clement V had excommunicated him, enthusiastically attended Bruce's coronation, captured Cupar Castle for the new king, and, in the month of Bruce's setback at Methven (June 1306), was captured at Cupar and clapped in irons at Wessex. After Bannockburn Bruce exchanged the earl of Hereford for his wife, his daughter, his sister Mary, and Bishop Wishart. Almost blind and very old, Robert Wishart died on 26 November 1316.*

decided to concentrate all his energies on a sustained guerilla campaign that would bewilder and demoralise the relatively immobile army of occupation. Soon he was able to test his campaign plan in the wild countryside of Glen Trool in Galloway. In April 1307 he ambushed John Mowbray's cavalry in the glen, inflicting a defeat severe enough to re-establish his military credibility and open up the way to the north.

On 10 May he passed an even sterner test. Greatly outnumbered by the army of the experienced Aymer de Valence, Bruce nevertheless out-manoeuvred him at Loudon Hill near Kilmarnock. By confining de Valence to an area unsuitable for his cavalry Bruce forced his enemy to flee to Bothwell. Almost immediately this was followed up by the defeat of the earl of Gloucester who, in turn, fled

Cruachan with the result that Mac-Dougall's men were sandwiched on a hillside while the two parts of Bruce's army closed in on them. When it was too close for comfort and Mac-Dougall's men fled across the river Awe, Bruce chased them to Dunstaffnage whose castle he then captured. With Buchan and Argyll in his control Bruce let his brother Edward get on with the job of taming Galloway. It was done with a bloody flourish.

Now that he had a country to be king of, Bruce held his first parliament —at St Andrews on 16–17 March 1309. Here the majority of the Scottish *communitas* endorsed him as the legitimate king of Scotland. In two years King Robert I had achieved an enormous amount by personal magnetism, tactical brilliance, and intelligent use of the respite gained by the death of Edward I and the indolence of Edward II. However, Lothian still had to be taken and the English held castles of immense strategic importance including Edinburgh and Stirling.

In 1310 and 1311 Edward II campaigned in Scotland but, inevitably, was a mere shadow compared to the mighty substance of his father. Bruce's counter-campaigns in England were another matter, unleashing terror and destruction on the northern counties. Between 1311 and 1313 northern Englishmen had to pay huge sums of money to buy peace from the destructive Scots. And all the time Bruce was relentlessly recovering the Scottish castles from the English. On the night

*   *   *

ABOVE RIGHT: *Kildrummy Castle, Grampian. After defeat at Methven and near-capture at Dalry, Bruce sent his queen Elizabeth and 12-year-old daughter Marjory to Kildrummy Castle which Neil Bruce helped to hold for his brother. In September 1306 the earl of Pembroke took Kildrummy (today the most complete 13th-century secular building in Scotland) and Edward I took his revenge by executing many of Bruce's supporters, including his brother.*

RIGHT: *Neil Bruce was hung, drawn and beheaded at Berwick-upon-Tweed, whose castle and fortifications (left) had been provided by Edward I after his capture of the town in 1296. Bruce's sister Mary and Countess Isabella of Buchan were displayed in cages at, respectively, Roxburgh and Berwick castles. Bruce's wife and daughter were put in separate prisons.*

ABOVE: *Glen Trool, in Galloway. When Bruce, after hiding on Rathlin island off the Irish coast, returned to his confiscated earldom of Carrick in February 1307 even his tenants were afraid to back him openly against Edward I. Accepting that the English would always outnumber him, Bruce determined to outmanoeuvre them whenever possible and decided to demonstrate his ability in a sustained guerilla campaign. In April 1307, in rugged Glen Trool in Galloway, he ambushed John Mowbray's small mounted force, thus beginning his war with a victory that cleared his way northward.*

FACING PAGE, ABOVE: *Caerlaverock Castle, 7 miles from Dumfries, was one of the strongest in south-west Scotland. In 1300 Edward I's 3,000-strong army* took two days, according to the old French poem "Le Siège de Karlaverok", to take it from 60 men. As long as the English commanded the Solway Firth the castles of Caerlaverock and Dumfries could withstand such as Edward Bruce's summer campaign of 1308. In July 1312 Robert the Bruce himself took charge of the assault and the two garrisons surrendered early the next year. Today Caerlaverock is possibly Scotland's finest medieval secular ruin.*

FACING PAGE, BELOW: *In the wars of independence Stirling Castle, gateway to the north, was of critical importance as Scotland's greatest stronghold. In 1296 Edward I occupied the castle; in 1297 Wallace, the victor of Stirling Bridge, captured it; in 1304 Edward I reoccupied it.*

of 7 January 1313 he led his men through the bitterly cold moat protecting Perth and was the second man over the wall. Such personal demonstrations of courageous involvement were always a main factor in endearing him to his adoring men.

By the beginning of 1314 the castles were falling one by one to the Scots. In February it was Roxburgh. In March it was Edinburgh. Stirling, however, was still garrisoned by the English under Sir Philip Mowbray. To the annoyance of King Robert his brother Edward Bruce had made an agreement with Stirling's English governor whereby the castle would be surrendered if the English had not

THE BATTLE OF BANNOCKBURN
23rd JUNE 1314 [first phase]

Stirling Castle

KING'S PARK

Cambuskenneth Abbey

River Forth

Roman Road

The Carse

Marshes

Livilands Bog

Probable mean tidal limit

CLIFFORD AND BEAUMONT LIGHT CAVALRY

Highest point of spring tides

KING EDWARD LEADING THE MAIN BODY OF CAVALRY AND FOOT

N

SMALL FOLK

Coxet Hill

MORAY

St Ninian's Church

DOUGLAS

KEITH LIGHT CAVALRY

NEW PARK

KING ROBERT

EDWARD BRUCE

BORESTONE ROTUNDA SITE

Milton Bog

BANNOCK BURN GORGE

BANNOCK PARK

Pits and Spikes

GLOUCESTER AND HEREFORD VANGUARD CAVALRY

MAIN BODY OF THE ENGLISH FROM FALKIRK

ROBERT BRUCE FAMILY TREE

KING MALCOLM CEANN-MOR — SAINT MARGARET OF ENGLAND

EDGAR — DAVID I (The Saint)

HENRY (Earl of Huntingdon)

WILLIAM (The Lion) — MALCOLM — DAVID (Earl of Northumberland)

ALEXANDER II — JOHN — MARGARET — ISABEL

ALEXANDER III — DEVORGUILLA — ROBERT BRUCE (5th Lord of Annandale)

MARGARET — JOHN BALLIOL — ALIANORA — ROBERT BRUCE

MARGARET (Maid of Norway) — JOHN COMYN — ROBERT BRUCE

ROBERT THE
BRUCE
KING
OF
SCOTS

1306-1329

relieved it by Midsummer Day. Bruce immediately saw that this would give the English an opportunity to gather their forces at a specific point and that he must either abandon the siege of the castle or defend it in pitched battle. Up to that moment all his success had been achieved precisely by avoiding pitched battles with the English.

Both sides knew that this, then, was going to be a crucial encounter, a decisive test of strength. If Edward II could not combine the might of feudal England to relieve one castle by a specific date then he would be revealed as a complete failure. If Bruce,

★   ★   ★

LEFT: C. d'O. Pilkington Jackson's equestrian bronze of Bruce was erected at the Borestone site at Bannockburn and unveiled by HM the Queen on 24 June 1964—the 650th anniversary of the victory. The inset map shows how the English and Scottish forces were deployed on 23 June 1314.

BELOW LEFT: Bruce had his battle headquarters at the Borestone. Though subsequently fragmented, it was originally a massive boulder with a socket in which Bruce is said to have placed his standard. The site is marked by this adjacent cairn, erected by the ancient Merchant Guild of the Burgh of Stirling in 1957 from funds raised by public subscription.

ABOVE RIGHT: Cambuskenneth Abbey (founded by David I c. 1140) was Bruce's supply depot at Bannockburn. Earl David of Atholl, outraged by Sir Edward Bruce's seduction of his sister, chose the night before the battle for his revenge: he attacked the abbey, killing Sir William of Airth, officer in charge. In 1326 the first Scottish parliament to include both Scottish nobility and burgh representatives met at Cambuskenneth Abbey, where it recognised David Bruce as King Robert's successor.

RIGHT: Stirling Castle was blockaded by Edward Bruce in the summer of 1313, and Sir Philip Mowbray, the English governor, agreed to surrender if he had not been relieved by Midsummer Day of 1314. It was while on their way to the relief of Stirling that the English forces under Edward II were intercepted by Bruce and his army at Bannockburn, below Stirling. After the battle Bruce dismantled the fortifications to render Stirling Castle useless to the English, and the present Renaissance structure evolved under James III, James IV and James V as a royal Stuart residence.

BANNOCKBVRN
A.D. 1314.

the master of guerilla warfare, could not for once publicly demonstrate his strength in a pre-arranged pitched battle in his own kingdom then he would lose not only Stirling, the gateway to the north, but his hard-won reputation as an invincible battler. Both sides had everything to lose. Neither side intended to leave anything to chance.

Edward II's greatest advantage was in the number of trained fighting men who were feudally obliged to him. Bruce, on the other hand, had military genius on his side and he planned the battle accordingly. He began in March to drill his troops in the Torwood and he chose the perfect

site for blocking the expected English advance on Stirling Castle. Bruce planted his men in the dense wood of the New Park and set his standard in the Borestone there. This meant that he had impassable scrub on his right, the stream-riddled and boggy Carse on his left, Stirling Castle behind him, and the Bannock Burn, which Edward II would have to cross, before him. In itself the narrow Bannock Burn was not a formidable obstacle but Bruce had it made so with ditches and cruelly-placed calthrops—four-pointed booby-traps that always landed spike-upwards to penetrate the feet of advancing cavalry. To get past the Scots, Bruce reckoned, Edward II

would be forced on to the Carse and there his numerical superiority and heavy cavalry would be of little use to him.

Edward II and his vast feudal host marched into Edinburgh on 17 June 1314, stopped five days to collect supplies at Leith, then had a 22-mile forced march to Falkirk. On Saturday 23 June 1314 they were advancing up the old Roman road from Falkirk to take up their positions for the forthcoming battle. Bruce, on his Highland pony, rode out in front of his men to see for himself the spectacle of the huge English army and to further assess his own position.

It must have been an awesome sight. The English army totalled some 20,000 men of whom 2,000 were heavy cavalry; 17,000 were archers and spear-wielding foot soldiers; and 1,000 were anti-Bruce fanatics including the Comyns and the Mac-Dougalls. By contrast Bruce's own army comprised only 5,500 trained men plus 2,000 untrained volunteers whom Barbour called the small folk. Against the English horsemen with their chain-mail and their armour and their quilted mounts, Bruce had only 500 light cavalry under Sir Alexander Keith. Against the thousands of experienced English archers, Bruce only a few from Ettrick Forest.

However Bruce had a definite plan. His army was divided into four divisions: *first* the men of Moray under their earl Randolph; *second* the men of Galloway, Aberdeen and the southeast Highlands under Edward Bruce; *third* the men of Renfrew under Sir James Douglas (knighted on the eve of battle) and Bruce's son-in-law Walter Stewart; *fourth* the men of Carrick and the Highlanders under Bruce himself. They would advance in echelon with himself bringing up the rear. They would deploy their spearmen in dense, outward-facing circles and these *schiltrons* would bristle forwards like huge metallic hedgehogs. The small folk would wait behind Coxet Hill until needed lest their inexperienced zeal upset Bruce's military preparations.

All these painstaking plans might have been ruined, however, if Bruce had not still possessed in abundance his personal courage in battle. As he surveyed the enemy army, axe in hand, the crown and leather hat that covered his bascinet clearly showed he was the king of Scots. Sir Henry de Bohun, a young distinguished

English knight, saw a glorious opportunity for immortality: if he killed the Scottish king in single combat he could cut the heart out of the Scottish army. With his 12-ft long lance at the ready he urged his charger towards Bruce who waited until the last possible moment then jerked his pony aside. As de Bohun careered past the unscathed pony and royal rider Bruce split open his skull, armour and all, and broke his axe shaft doing so.

When he returned to his men the divisional commanders pointed out, with alarm, what the consequences might have been in the dramatic fight. By risking his life Bruce was risking his country's future. The king disagreed. What he lamented most was his broken axe shaft. Yet he knew, too,

*   *   *

FACING PAGE: *Mural of the battle of Bannockburn by William Hole. Born in Salisbury in 1846, William Hole studied in Italy and was later responsible for a series of historical murals in Edinburgh including this painting in the Scottish National Portrait Gallery.*

ABOVE RIGHT: *Drawing of Bruce and de Bohun from John Fordun's* Scotichronicon. *Before the battle commenced Henry de Bohun saw Bruce isolated from his men, sitting on a Highland pony, and armed only with a hand-axe. In an impetuous attempt to kill the Scottish king the English knight rode forward with his lance at the ready for a hit, but Bruce waited until the last moment, then jerked his horse to the side. As Barbour put it, "Schyr Henry myssit the noble king"—but Bruce did not miss Sir Henry. With one fearsome smash of his axe he split open de Bohun's head. Bruce was criticised for taking risks but his personal example of bravery and skill had its intended effect on his men. This 15th-century drawing, which has Stirling and the castle in the background, commemorates the encounter which every Scottish schoolboy knows in the lines: "Bruce and de Bohun fightin' for the croon :| Bruce took his battle-axe and knocked de Bohun doon."*

RIGHT: *The Monymusk Reliquary. This small casket, made about 100 years after the death of Columba in 597, contained a relic of the saint. Around 1211 King William the Lion presented it to Arbroath Abbey on condition that the monks would take it to the Scottish army in time of battle. At Bannockburn Chancellor Bernard de Linton was, as Abbot of Arbroath, responsible for making its inspiring presence known to the soldiers.*

15

that his personal example of courage would once again inspire his men to see if they could do in battle what their king had done.

On Sunday morning, 24 June 1314, Bruce addressed his troops in a speech whose words were preserved by his Chancellor Bernard de Linton who, as Abbot of Arbroath, was present at Bannockburn as bearer of the Monymusk Reliquary. Bruce began by stressing that his men faced not just an army but a national crisis. "My lords, my people", he began, "accustomed to enjoy that full freedom for which in times gone by the kings of Scotland have fought many a battle! For eight years or more I have struggled with much labour for my right to the kingdom and for honourable liberty. I have lost brothers, friends and kinsmen. Your own kinsmen have been made captive, and bishops and priests are locked in prison. Our country's nobility has poured forth its blood in war."

Then, with his patriotic credentials established, Bruce turned the attentions of his men to the enemy: "Those barons you can see before you, clad in mail, are bent upon destroying me and

obliterating my kingdom, nay, our whole nation. They do not believe that we can survive. They glory in their warhorses and equipment." Inspiring his men to a crusade of a battle he contrasted the mechanical strength of the English with the spiritual strength of the Scottish army. "For us", Bruce said, "the name of the Lord must be our hope of victory in battle. This day is a day of rejoicing: the birthday of John the Baptist. With our Lord Jesus Christ as commander, Saint Andrew and the martyr Saint Thomas shall fight today with the saints of Scotland for the honour of their country and their nation." As a practical afterthought Bruce promised a general pardon for "all those who fight manfully for the kingdom of our fathers".

In Bruce's single-handed dismissal of de Bohun the Scots had seen a great warrior king in action. In his address to them before the battle they beheld a great patriot king. As the Scots emerged from the New Park in the dawn of Midsummer Day they knelt to receive the blessing of the Abbot of Inchaffray. Edward II, frustrated in the past at the exclusive Scottish reliance on guerilla tactics, thought

the Scots were quailing at the prospect of a pitched battle. "These men kneel for mercy", Edward II gloated. A wiser man told him that their plea for mercy was addressed to God and not the English king.

Besides, Edward II had already sown the seeds of his own failure on the peatbogs of the Carse. On Midsummer's eve the English cavalry had crossed the Bannock Burn and had taken up a position on the Carse between Pelstream Burn and Bannock Burn. Edward II thought this force would wait in readiness until the Scots retreated from his massive frontal attack. Then his cavalry would cut down the scattering Scots. Instead,

*   *   *

ABOVE: *Arbroath Abbey, Tayside. This 13th-century abbey, founded in 1178, assumed a critical importance during the reign of Robert the Bruce. In 1311 King Robert made his Chancellor, Bernard de Linton, Abbot of Arbroath. An assembly of the Scottish nobility, meeting at Arbroath Abbey in April 1320, agreed on a common policy of protest against papal disapproval of their king. The result was the Declaration of Arbroath, 1320.*

Edward II, like de Valence at Loudon Hill, had fallen into Bruce's trap by confining his mobile force in an impossibly narrow area. When the four Scottish divisions—with Edward Bruce in the van and Robert the Bruce in the rear—advanced in echelon the earl of Gloucester attempted to initiate the crushing frontal assault. Not only did Edward Bruce's *schiltrons* keep advancing but they repulsed the English, killing Gloucester himself, a more able military mind than Edward II, in the process.

It was the English, not the Scots, who were beginning to fall back. When English archers opened fire on the Scottish left flank Bruce immediately brought in Keith's cavalry to drive the celebrated bowmen from the field. Then, at the critical moment, the king himself brought his reserve division surging forward so explosively that the rapidly retreating English became unavoidable targets for their own back line of archers. Edward II decided he had had enough and rushed for the safety of his garrison in Stirling Castle. But Sir Philip Mowbray would not let him in so the English king had to flee towards Dunbar.

The knowledge that their king had deserted them left the English army with little fighting spirit so when, suddenly, the small folk appeared from Coxet Hill the English were horrified. To their battle-weary eyes this looked like a wild attack by fresh Scottish troops. The English right flank tried to follow the direction of their humiliated king. The English centre headed suicidally for the waters of the Forth. The English left fell back, like human debris, into the Bannock Burn. Not only were the English totally defeated in pitched battle, but Bruce had grabbed valuable hostages like the earl of Hereford whom he exchanged for his wife, daughter, and friend the Bishop of Glasgow. As for Edward II's mighty train of equipment—all £200,000 of it was abandoned and left to the Scots.

Although it was to be fourteen years before the war was officially over there was no doubt that Bruce and his men had won its most decisive battle. He was unquestionably in control of his kingdom. He had shown that he could defeat the English by guerilla tactics or in pitched battle if need be. He had his wife back (she was to produce a male heir, David, in 1324) and an unshakeable grasp of his throne. Just as he had used the timely death of

Edward I to consolidate so he used the utter defeat of Edward II to assert his strength even more forcefully.

And yet, at a time when as many troops as possible were needed in Scotland, Bruce authorised his brother Edward to leave Ayr in May 1315 on an Irish campaign: there was always James Douglas at home. Nothing could diminish the Black Douglas's fighting spirit. In February 1316 he flamboyantly distinguished himself in a ferocious encounter with the English at Skaithmuir near Coldstream, then topped this exploit by mounting several successful assaults on would-be Border raiders from England.

In Ireland the Scottish force, undoubtedly infused with the spirit of Bannockburn, gained a series of victories that ended in the coronation of Edward Bruce, king of Ireland, in May 1316 at Dunkald. Historically

the Scots had originated in northern Ireland and King Robert might have been reciprocating an ethnic gesture by establishing a second kingdom, under brother Edward, which would be an effective base for launching attacks on Edward II. In the winter of 1316, therefore, King Robert joined King Edward in Ireland. What appalled the brother monarchs was not the armed opposition they met in Ireland but the presence of plague and famine. So in 1317 Bruce returned

* * *

ABOVE: *It was to Pope John XXII that the Declaration of Arbroath was addressed, though it was not until January 1324 that he recognised Robert the Bruce as king of Scotland. This 15th-century miniature from* The Travels of Sir John Mandeville *shows Pope John receiving emissaries from the Greek Church.*

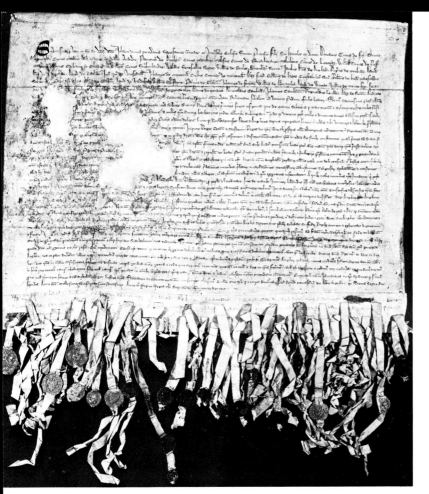

to his own kingdom where his influential presence was needed.

On the night of 1 April 1318, thanks to the help of English burgess Peter of Spalding, Douglas and his men surmounted the fortified walls of Berwick, took control of the town and besieged the castle which, when it eventually surrendered three months later, was put into the hands of Walter Stewart. This impressive victory was followed by the capture of three Northumberland castles: Wark, Harbottle, and Mitford. These achievements, accompanied by punitive raids, swung things still further in King Robert's favour.

In October 1318, however, Bruce heard that brother Edward had been killed, and his army defeated, at the battle of Dunkald. Apart from the personal impact of the loss of a brother this fraternal death had the practical effect of raising the question of the succession again. It was settled on Robert Stewart, born in March 1316 as his mother Marjory Bruce died after falling from a horse.

Edward II was ready for another tilt at Bruce. Yet even with 8,000 men he could not recapture Berwick Castle. Douglas and Moray knew it would be foolish to meet this large army in pitched battle so they took to raiding Yorkshire. The only opposition they met, composed of clergymen and civilians from York, was cut down at Myton-on-Swale (also known as the Chapter of Myton because of the clerical deaths involved). Edward II was persuaded to remove himself from the Border and in his absence Douglas

★   ★   ★

ABOVE LEFT: *The Declaration of Arbroath, dated 6 April 1320 "at the Monastery of Arbroath in Scotland". This masterly document, probably composed in Latin by Bruce's Chancellor Bernard de Linton, Abbot of Arbroath, has become the classic declaration of Scottish independence: "For so long as one hundred men remain alive, we shall never under any conditions submit to the domination of the English. It is not for glory or riches or honours that we fight, but only for liberty, which no good man will consent to lose but with his life."*

LEFT: *The obverse of a Robert I silver penny, showing the king with sceptre and crown. Such coins were probably issued after Bannockburn as before that victory Bruce was not sufficiently established to deal with national finance.*

unleashed destruction on the west side of the Pennines.

As a result of this latest failure Edward II agreed, on 25 December 1319, to a two-year truce. But having failed to impose his will on Bruce by force Edward II still persisted in his propaganda, continuing to emphasise the iniquity of Bruce to the Pope. Since his sacrilegious murder of Comyn, Bruce's name had been anathema to the papacy and Pope John XXII followed Clement V in regarding the Scottish king as an unrepentant sinner. When four Scottish bishops ignored a papal summons they were therefore excommunicated along with their king. However, the Scots, having fought so hard for their independence, were ready to make a declaration of their case to anyone. Even an unsympathetic Pope.

At a meeting at Arbroath Abbey in April 1320 the Scottish nobility, the *communitas*, unanimously agreed to endorse a letter of protest which was almost certainly composed, in memorable Latin prose, by Bruce's Chancellor Bernard de Linton, Abbot of Arbroath. This celebrated Declaration of Arbroath, dated 6 April 1320, was sent to Pope John XXII in Avignon and though he acknowledged receipt of the letter he took until January 1324 to recognise Robert the Bruce as king of Scotland.

In the Declaration Bruce is described as a king "who, that he might

*   *   *

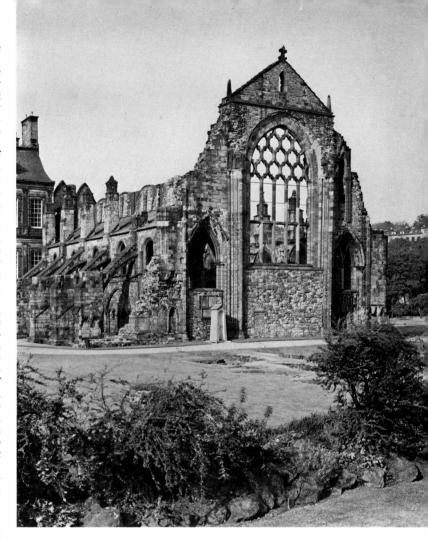

ABOVE RIGHT: *Holyrood Abbey, the 13th-century Augustinian monastery where on 17 March 1328 the Treaty of Edinburgh (ratified at Northampton on 4 May) was concluded. When 14-year-old Edward III succeeded his deposed father in 1327 he had to face the consequences of Edward II's consistent refusal to recognise Bruce as king of Scotland. Bruce's army invaded England and reduced the teenage king to tears by their hit-and-run tactics at Stanhope Park. Next came a campaign of destruction throughout Northumberland and Edward III's council of regency agreed to treat for peace. Bruce was on his sickbed at Holyrood Abbey when the treaty was concluded there.*

RIGHT: *The Treaty of Edinburgh. In it Edward III renounced all claims to the Scottish throne, Bruce was recognised as king, and a marriage was arranged between Bruce's son and Edward III's sister. As far as Bruce was concerned the war was over. He had just over a year to live.*

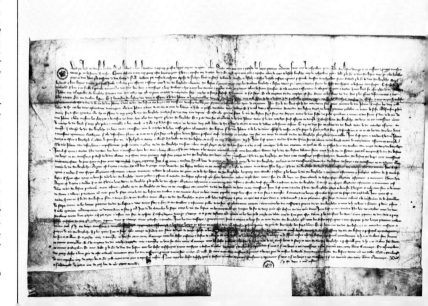

ABOVE: *Dunfermline Abbey, Fife. Since Malcolm Canmore's time this 12th-century Benedictine abbey had replaced Iona as the sepulchre of the Scottish kings and in 1329 Bruce was buried beside his queen (who predeceased him by two years) before the high altar. In 1560 the Reformers ruined much of the abbey and the king's tomb was lost until 1818 when workmen discovered a vaulted chamber containing Bruce's skeleton wrapped in sheet lead.*

LEFT: *Bruce's skeleton, its sternum sawn through when the heart was removed, was reinterred below the present pulpit and its resting place is now marked by this porphyry slab and monumental brass.*

FACING PAGE: *Melrose Abbey, in the Borders. In 1322 Edward II's retreating army sacked this 12th-century Cistercian abbey and at a special parliament at Scone in 1325 Bruce concerned himself with its restoration. Five years later his heart, which had been brought back to Scotland from Spain, was probably buried here.*

free his people and heritage from the hands of the enemy, rose like another Joshua or Maccabeus, and cheerfully endured toil and weariness, hunger and peril". And to emphasise that Bruce was king by common consent and no tyrant the Declaration assured the Pope that "were he to abandon the task to which he has set his hand or to show any disposition to subject us or our realm to the King of England or the English, we would instantly strive to expel him as our enemy and . . . choose another King to rule over us".

Having said this, the author of the Declaration reached the memorable climax of his argument in the celebrated passage beginning "*Quia, quamdiu centum ex nobis vivi remanserint*": "For so long as one hundred men remain alive, we shall never under any conditions submit to the domination of the English. It is not for glory or riches or honour that we fight, but